/95

God Is Here—
Let's Celebrate!

GOD IS HERE
LET'S CELEBRATE!

In 39 Meditations
Based on Psalms

by

Leslie F. Brandt

Publishing House
St. Louis   London

Third Printing 1970

Concordia Publishing House, St. Louis, Missouri
Concordia Publishing House Ltd., London, E. C. 1
© 1969 Concordia Publishing House
Library of Congress Catalog Card No. 73-89877
MANUFACTURED IN THE UNITED STATES OF AMERICA

Contents

Preface

This is a sequel to *Good Lord, Where Are You?* Though the selections in that volume are called "paraphrases," they are actually prayers based on specific psalms or portions of psalms. So also with this volume. Here is what the psalmist might be saying if he were living in the 20th century. Living in the 20th century, as we are, he would be saying it within the context of New Testament Christianity. True, the Christ name is not used; the word "Gospel" is not included; the Messianic import of the psalms is not noted. Yet these prayers are those of the Christian on this side of the Easter event — one whose every approach to God must be by way of God revealed through Jesus Christ. After all, this is exactly the Christian's approach when he prays the Old Testament psalms themselves.

The first volume portrays the insatiable hunger of the psalmist, or the 20th-century Christian, for God — his perplexities and frustrations as he grapples for some sense of God's presence and power in this discordant world. This sequel is an attempt at a positive response. It places the major emphasis on the praise psalms — manifesting the confidence that "God is here" and is calling upon His children to celebrate this truth in word and deed.

Doubts and perplexities continue to assail the disciples of Christ. We may honestly and openly express them in our conversations with God. At the same time we can lay claim to His promises and demonstrate our faith in celebration of His presence in our world today.

God is here — let's celebrate!

Leslie F. Brandt

7

PSALM 3

O God, the obstacles that confront me today
    are so many!
And even as they press in upon me,
    there are people about me
      who laugh at my childlike dependence on You.
They claim that my faith is futile,
    that God is not interested
      in my petty problems.

But, God, You have surrounded me with Your love.
You envelop me with concern
    and undergird me with grace.
When I reach out for You,
    You are close enough to hear and to respond

Whether I am awake or asleep,
    You are near to me and will watch over me.
I do not have to be afraid
    of these problems that assail me.
The conflicts of my life
    will not separate me from You.

I constantly seek Your deliverance
    from all that hurts or hinders.
You are able to rid my life
    of everything that may threaten
      my relationship to You.
You will in Your own good time set me free
    from every human fault and frailty.

But even while I seek Your ultimate deliverance,
    help me to sense Your presence and power
    in the midst of my many conflicts.

PSALM 5

Can You hear, O God, what I have to say?
Do You feel something of what I feel this morning?

I know, O God, that You are grieved
        by the selfishness of Your children.
The world You created seems to be falling apart.
Your creatures are living for themselves alone.
They are proud and self-sufficient.
They think they don't need You any longer.

I also know, O Lord, that I cannot exist
        without the assurance of Your eternal love.
Thus I commit myself once more
        to You and Your purposes.
Help me to walk in Your path for my life.
Give me the grace to overcome
        the many obstacles in the way.

The philosophies that come out of our world
        bear little resemblance
            to the truth You revealed to us.
They are subtle and seductive,
        and men are led astray
            by forked tongues and suave soft-sell.
Enable us to recognize them for what they are:
        shallow, superficial, ultimately destructive.

Those who follow You need not be dismayed.
They can sing and dance in the joy of their Lord.
You will continue to reveal Yourself to them
    and care for them
    and work out Your purposes
      in and through them.

PSALM 8

O God,
    how full of wonder and splendor You are!

I see the reflections of Your beauty
    and hear the sounds of Your majesty
      wherever I turn.
Even the babbling of babes
    and the laughter of children
      spell out Your name in indefinable syllables.

When I gaze into star-studded skies
    and attempt to comprehend the vast distances,
I contemplate in utter amazement
    my Creator's concern for me.
I am dumbfounded that You
    should care personally about me.

And yet You have made me in Your image.
You have called me Your son.
You have ordained me as Your priest
    and chosen me to be Your servant.

You have assigned to me
   the fantastic responsibility
      of carrying on Your creative activity.

O God,
   how full of wonder and splendor You are!

PSALM 11

I am frightened by the insecurities about me.
I am sorely tempted to run for my life,
      to take refuge in foolish escapades
         that dim the vision and drug the soul.

There is no escape
      from the realities of this fractured world.
When we awaken from our stupor
      or return to sobriety,
      they are ever present
         to haunt and oppress us.

But there is a place of refuge.
God is in our midst.
He is aware of the fears and apprehensions
      of His beloved children.
He may not always rid us of our fears.
He does promise to face them with us,
      to make them stepping-stones to faith,
         to use them to draw us closer to Himself.

I need not worry overmuch
      about the distortions of this world.

I do need to be aware that God is here
and allow Him through me
to reveal Himself to His world.

PSALM 13

O God, sometimes You seem so far away.
I cannot in this moment sense Your presence
or feel Your power.

The darkness about me is stifling.
This depression is suffocating.
How long, O God,
do I have to live in this void?
O God, how long?

Break into this black night, O God;
fill in this vast emptiness.
Enter into my conflict
lest I fall never to rise again.

I continue to trust in Your ever-present love.
I shall again discover true joy
in my relationship to You.
I will proclaim Your praises, my Lord,
for You will never let me go.

PSALM 14

How foolish it is to deny the existence of God
    or to say that "God is dead"!
And yet there are many who do so.
They say it in the way they live
    if not in the words they speak.

Our great God is forever searching for those
    who will open their lives to Him.
He is not looking for such
    in verbal professions alone
        but in the way men live and act.

He sees denial and rebellion in the lives
    of all men.
What good they do is tainted by sin
    and self-centeredness.
They are more apt to be destructive
    than creative.
How foolish they are
    if they neglect to surrender their lives to God!

It is obvious that God works
    through those who trust Him,
    through those who dedicate their lives
        to His service.
It is they who are set free from self-glory
    to enjoy and to serve the living God.
They can truly celebrate
    the eternal presence of God.

PSALM 16

Sustain me, O God,
    for I am anchoring my faith in You.
I say it again,
    "You are my Lord;
    when I am estranged from You,
        I have nothing that is of any real worth."

The significant and contributive people
    of this world
        are those who know You.
They are the individuals I must respect.
Those who make lesser things
    their ultimate concern
        are investing in eventual trouble and grief.
I cannot worship their idols
    or respect their objectives.

I have chosen to make God my ultimate concern.
He is the Pilot of my ship.
Thus the course before me will lead
    to ultimate fulfillment.
I am guaranteed an inheritance of infinite value.

I look to God as my chief counselor.
Even in the darkest of night
    He is ready to teach and guide me.
I need only to recognize His perpetual presence.
Because He continually surrounds me,
    I shall not lose my way.

Is it any wonder that I am happy?
Even my humanity, my tangible body,
      rests in the blessed realization
            of this security.
He will keep even my human self
      from the destructive clutch of evil.

You do show me the paths I must take.
Within Your all-embracing presence
      there is genuine fulfillment.
In my relationship with You
      I discover incomparable and eternal joy.

PSALM 18

It is no wonder that I love You, O God.
You have granted me a security
      that I could never find
            among the things of this world.

You have erased from my life the fear of death.
What follows the grave is not my fearful concern.
The traumatic experiences of this life
      cannot destroy me.
You are never out of reach
      but are ever aware
            of my problems and conflicts.

How great and all-powerful is my God!
The quaking of the earth,
      the shaking of the mountains,
      the blackness of the night,

the beauty of the heavens,
the lightning that crisscrosses our skies,
the oceans that lash against our shores:
this and much more bear witness
    to the majesty of my God.
And this is the God who is concerned about me.
He reaches into my distraught life
    to heal my wounds.
He encompasses me with eternal love.
He abides with me even in the midst
    of conflict or calamity.
He sets me free from self-idolatry
    so I may serve His creatures about me.
He shields me from the forces that are intent
    on my destruction.
I am His delight and heart's desire.
It is no wonder, O God, that I love You.

Can there be any God but this God that I love?
He surrounds me with His strength
    and clothes me with His grace.
He puts into my hands gifts for relay to others.
He entrusts me with tasks
    far beyond my human abilities
        and enables me to carry them out.
He ordains me as His son and servant
    destined to accomplish His purposes
        amongst the peoples of this world.

It is thus that I celebrate God's presence
    in my life and world.
God is not dead; He lives.
I rejoice in His concern and love for me.
I will proclaim, O Lord,
    Your praises to anyone who will listen to me.
I will sing and shout and dance
    in the joy of knowing that You are my God.

PSALM 19

Wherever I am, wherever I go,
    I can sense something of the power of God.
The grandeur of the mountains,
    the vastness of the oceans,
    the breathtaking wonder of interstellar space:
    all this proclaims
        the glory and majesty of God.
Even amid the clutter of our cities,
    built and abused by the hands of men,
    there are reflections of divine splendor.
Heaven's silence or earth's clamor
    may not be very articulate.
Yet God's voice can be heard.
He makes His presence known
    throughout the world.

God has made for man a path he is to walk in.
In His will there is order and purpose.
He has proclaimed and demonstrated eternal truth
    through the lips and lives of His children.
There are set before the sons of men
    precepts and principles which direct
    His creatures in the way of peace and joy.
He has given meaning to life,
    goal and objective to this existence.
Therein is the answer to man's inner need,
    the fulfillment of his deepest longings.
These things are more precious
      and of greater value

than anything a man could ever experience
or even dare to imagine.

This is the course which I must travel.
It is not easy; I make so many mistakes.
I am plagued with faults and obsessions.
O God, forbid that these should destroy me.
Set me free from their tenacious hold on me.
Encompass me with Your love and grace
that these things may not stand
between You and me.

O God,
these are the thoughts
that crowd my heart today.
Accept them and respond to them,
and enable me to realize anew
the security and serenity
of Your loving presence in my life.

PSALM 21

O God,
in the grace and strength that You daily grant,
Your servant finds reason for celebration.
You have truly fulfilled his innermost longings.
You have responded to his deepest needs.

He asked for security,
and You encompassed him with love.
He looked to You for life,
and You granted him life eternal.

19

He sought for identity,
    and You adopted him as Your son.
Whatever is of value and worth in his life
    has come by way of Your rich blessings.
His heart is glad in the realization
    of Your eternal presence.
He knows that he will never lose Your love.

I raise my voice in praise, O God,
    because no one can separate me from You.
Though circumstances threaten me
    and my own obsessions entangle me,
        You will never let me go.
Your great power is sufficient to set me free
    from these things that hurt my soul.
If I put my trust in You,
    You will not allow them to destroy me.
I find so many reasons for praising You, O God.

PSALM 22

O God, why have You left me?
Why are You so far from me?
I can no longer feel You near.
I reach desperately for You,
    but I cannot find You.

I know You are holy and all-righteous
    and everywhere present.
The saints of past years believed in You
    and trusted You.
You responded to their cries.

They sought for You, and they found You.
It is no wonder that Your praises
    were constantly on their lips.

But I feel as empty and insignificant
    as a bag full of wind.
I don't really expect men's plaudits,
    but I so sorely feel their criticism.
I risk all in following
    what I feel to be Your will for me;
    yet even my friends fail to support me,
        and they actually turn against me.
"He thinks he's doing God's will," they say.
"But he'll be sorry he made that decision."

I believe that You were with me
    from the very beginning of my life.
I know that You have cared for me
    through these many years.
But, God, I need You now.
I am in trouble,
    and I can't find You or feel You to be near.

O God,
    I feel in this moment as if I am falling apart.
Nothing seems to make sense anymore.
Everything I attempt to do ends in failure.
I feel inferior and weak.
Those I have tried to serve
    are actually gloating
        over my flops and failures.
I know, O God, that much of it
    is a matter of my foolish feelings.
The fact is, You are not far off.
You know both my feelings and my failings.
Yet You love me and accept me.
You will save me — even from myself.

Thus I will continue to sing Your praises.
In spite of or in scorn of my feelings
	I will celebrate Your loving presence.
As despicable as I may feel at times,
	You do not despise me, nor will You leave me.
Your love is personal, and it is eternal.

Nor will You despise or ignore the afflictions
	that plague Your many children.
Your sons and servants are precious to You.
Even when they fail You, You will never fail them.
You hear their cries and feel their pain
	and are ever ready to support them
		in their conflicts.

I dedicate myself anew to You, O Lord.
I will serve You
	whatever the cost or the consequence.
You are my God.
Regardless of my feelings
	of insignificance and inadequacy,
I will praise Your name and proclaim Your love
	to men all about me.

PSALM 24

Let us never forget that this world
	and everything in it belongs to God.
But not all of this world's citizens
	recognize or give allegiance to their Creator.

Who are they who truly love and serve God?

It is they who discover and live
within His purposes for their lives.
It is they whose hearts and hands
are dedicated to His will for them.
It is they who turn away
from self-centered concerns
to live for others about them.
They are the ones who can count
on God's perpetual blessings.
They nevermore need to be concerned
about their personal salvation.
They have been delivered from such anxiety
to focus their efforts and endeavors
on communicating God's eternal love
to their fellowmen.

Let us look up and live!
God is present in all His glory and majesty.
Let us let go and celebrate!
Our loving Lord is here with us
and will manifest Himself through us.
We are the vehicles and vessels
of the King of kings.
We represent Him in all His saving power.
We are His beloved and empowered servants
in this world that He created.

PSALM 29

We need to give credit to whom credit is due.
God is alive,
and He deserves our perpetual praises.

There is reason for rejoicing.
There is a God to worship and love.

His beauty is manifest
    in the skies and the forests.
His power is represented
    in the sweep of the ocean.
His majesty is portrayed
    in the gigantic bodies
        suspended in our universe.
The wind and the rain, lightning and thunder,
    the creatures that inhabit our land,
    the flowers that brighten our lives:
        all this comes from God's hand.
The glory is not ours but God's.

Even the achievements of man's mind and hand
    come by way of the wisdom and power
        of the eternal God.
The contributions of science,
    the fields ripe for harvest,
    the control of our rivers,
    the activity in our cities,
    the establishment of our great institutions:
        these also reflect the glory of God.

Let us give credit to whom credit is due.
Let us rejoice in the God who blesses us.
Let us seek His grace to serve Him
    by serving others with the abundance
        that He bestows upon us.

PSALM 31

I am up a blind alley, Lord.
The props have been knocked out beneath me.
I feel as if I'm grappling with the wind
    for some support or security.
I've been pulled up short, Lord.
Now I realize how much I need
    something or someone
    beyond and above myself
      to give stability to my tenuous existence.
Maybe it was Your doing, Lord.
It is Your way of bringing me back to home port,
    of correcting my focus
    and reassessing my goals.

I return to You with empty hands, Lord.
You know well my sorry plight.
I did not find that secret treasure,
    that pearl of great price.
The bright lights that beckoned
    only led me astray.
I became entangled in the bonds of self-service.
Everything I touched turned to dust in my hands.

I despise myself today, Lord.
Even those I thought my friends
    turn their faces from me.
There is no place to go, nothing to cling to.
I can only come back to You
    and cast myself on Your loving mercy.

You are my God.
You have never let me out of Your sight.
Even when I strike out on my own,
    You pursue me and hold on to me.

I've stopped running, Lord.
From this point on
    I will dedicate my hours and days
        into Your loving hands.
I seek only Your guidance
    and the grace and strength
        to carry out Your purposes.
Restore me, O God,
    to Your program and design for my life.

Thank You for taking me back, Lord,
    for renewing my relationship with You.
I seek now to walk in Your course for me.
I shall abide forever in Your steadfast love.
I will proclaim Your praises
    and live out Your purposes.
Enable me to be faithful to You,
        whatever the consequences,
    and to celebrate Your love
        and communicate it to everyone around me.

PSALM 33

God is here—let's celebrate!
    with song and with dance,
    with stringed instruments and brass,
    with cymbals and drums,
    let us express our ecstatic joy
        in God's presence.

Let us celebrate with the old songs of praise.
Let us also create new songs
     that portray the eternal love of our God.

He did create this world.
He continues to permeate it with His love.
Even amongst its distortions,
     its frustrated and unbelieving children,
          He constantly carries out His purposes.
His plans for His world and its inhabitants
     are not obliterated by the foolishness of men.
His truth is not blotted out
     by the lethargy or lies
          of His apathetic creatures.
He continues to reign over us
     and to reveal Himself to us.

And God continues to create and to renew
     the world about us.
He does this through those who relate to Him,
     who rely on His ever-present love.
He delivers His children from the fear of death
     and through them gives life to this world.
God's love is sure and everlasting.
The hearts that are open to His love
     are filled with joy.
They truly find cause for celebration.

PSALM 37

It's high time we stop complaining
    about the dissipation of our world
    or the corruption of our society.
At the same time we eye with envy
    those ungodly characters
      who appear to have more fun
      or to be more successful than we are.

If we really trusted in God
    and were truly committed to His purposes,
    the world might be
      a great deal better off today.
God is in our world.
He is destined to be the source
    of our joy and well-being.
He is the fulfillment of our hearts' desires.
If we dedicate our lives to Him and His will,
    He will be able to work through us,
    to permeate this world's darkness
      with divine light.

Let's keep our cool and try to be patient.
Stop worrying about the apparent hopelessness
    of it all.
We only contribute to this despair
    by always being negative and defeatist.
God has not taken a vacation; He is here.
He has His own way of dealing
    with the instigators of corruption.

It will take time,
   but the victory is ultimately God's.
Those who live within God's will
   shall surely discover
      that His purposes prevail,
      that true joy and peace and security
         come from Him.

Let us wait on God and seek daily to obey Him.
He is our salvation and our security,
   and nothing in this world
      can take that away from us.
Let us calm our hostilities,
   overcome our anxieties,
      and walk in peace and love.

PSALM 41

I believe that he who gives of himself
   for the sake of others,
   who demonstrates genuine concern
   for those who are less fortunate,
      that he is especially blessed by God.
He is precious in God's eyes
   and is protected by Him.
Even as he faces the hatred of his enemies
   or the conflicts and illnesses
      of this existence,
   the Lord delivers and sustains him.

It is for this reason that I dare to claim
   God's gracious intervention on my behalf.

It is true that my sins are many.
I reach desperately for God's forgiving mercy.
I receive no comfort from many
    who I thought were my friends.
I could drop dead; they couldn't care less.
When we meet,
    their words are empty,
    their thoughts pregnant with suspicion.
When we part,
    they go out to spread their suspicions abroad,
        imagining the worst about me
        and whispering behind my back.

I can well imagine their conversation:
    "One would think he'd be
        beyond this sort of thing;
    and here he calls himself religious.
    Why, he's as bad as the worst of them.
    He's had it! He won't crawl out of this!"
Even the one person I trusted the most,
    in whom I confided,
    with whom I lovingly related,
    even he looks down his nose at me
    as one he would rather step on than support.
He no longer wants anything to do with me.

My loving God, You are truly gracious to me.
You have not cast me aside
    or allowed me to be destroyed.
You know that I honestly want to serve You.
And You have demonstrated
    Your acceptance and concern for me
        in sustaining me
        and drawing me even closer to Yourself.
May God be praised forever!

PSALM 43

O God,
    my life is cluttered up with conflicts.
And there are times
    when You seem so oblivious to it all.
The pitfalls before me, the weaknesses within me:
    all this is most depressing.
I feel as if I am groping in utter darkness.

Break into my darkness, O God.
Set me free from my hang-ups.
May these daily pressures
    that threaten to strangle me
        drive me to Your fountainhead of grace.
Then night will give way to the dawn,
    depression shall resolve into joy,
        and I shall sing Your praises once more.

O foolish spirit,
    why do you fret over so many things?
God is here!
He knows all about your troubles and trials.
Renew your faith in Him, and rejoice.

I shall rejoice!
No matter how black the night,
    God is my ever-present and eternal Hope.

PSALM 44

O God,
> I have heard so much about how close You were
>> to Your children throughout history.

They clobbered the enemy
> and credited You for their victories.

When they were defeated,
> they accepted their lot
>> as Your righteous judgment.

They assumed they were Your beloved charges
> and even accepted their afflictions
>> as from Your hand.

It was their persistent faith in You
> that held them together
>> through the crises of their lives.

And I am aware of how You have watched over me
> in the midst of my conflicts.

You have enabled me to overcome
> many of the obstacles in my life.

Even when I so miserably failed,
> You set me on my feet again
> and directed me on Your course for my life.

I am keenly aware of my incapabilities
> and inadequacies,
>> of how much I need You.

I know all this, Lord.

You have been an integral part
> of my life's experiences.

I am deeply grateful for Your care and concern.

But what about now?
I am on the spot—and I can't reach You.
It seems as if You have left the scene
    and I am left holding the bag.
I cry for help
    and hear only the echo of my own voice.
I grope about me
    and find insurmountable walls and dark corners.
The advice of my peers and superiors
    seems devoid of genuine love or concern.
O God, if You are truly my God,
    reveal Yourself to me now.
I simply cannot bear the shame and the pain
    of my problem.
Nobody around me can help me.
If people knew about it,
    they would only shun me.

I have not forgotten You, O God.
I do believe in You as I have been taught.
I worshiped You and sang Your praises
    when all was well.
I have dedicated my life
    to You and Your purposes.
Now I am in deep trouble.
I have no one else to turn to.

O God, listen to me.
Respond to my cry for help.
Deliver me from this terrible conflict
    before it destroys me.
Help me to sense Your loving concern.
Save me before it is too late.

PSALM 47

Clap your hands, stamp your feet!
Let your bodies and your voices
    explode with joy.
God is not some human concoction.
He is for real! And He is here!
Despite all attempts
      to rationalize Him out of existence,
    He is in our world,
      and He reigns over our universe.

The rulers of nations often ignore Him.
Men of learning often pass Him by.
The masses of His creatures substitute
      their own little gods in His place
    and worship the things they can see and feel.
There are others who build fortresses
    about themselves
    and manifest no need for God.

Our great God will not be ignored.
He will not remove Himself from our world.
Let us recognize His presence
    and fill the air with His praises.

PSALM 49

How foolish are the creatures of God!
They accumulate wealth
  and imagine themselves secure
    in possessions and property.
Or they utilize some inborn gift
  and dote on the plaudits of their peers.
They live for themselves alone
  and give no thought to eternity.
They claim that God is simply
  not necessary to their existence.
He is just a big thumb in the sky
  designed to pacify the weak and the childish.
They claim that man must be
  sufficient unto himself.
He doesn't need the extra baggage
  of faith or religion.

But when the riches melt away,
  health fails, talents wear thin,
    and remaining years become few,
  when no one honors them
    or expresses concern for them,
  then they stand naked and exposed
    in empty despair.
Their fortress is breached;
  they are flattened and defeated.
Life, what little of it there is left,
  no longer has meaning for them.
Then they may look desperately for the God
  whom they discarded in their youth.

Let us consider carefully the security
of a loving relationship to God.
Let us mouth His praises
and demonstrate in our lives
the eternal joy
of knowing and relating to Him.
We need not depend on this world's wealth
nor the accolades of men.
We need not fear the end of our days
upon this earth.
God is forever —
and so the souls of those
who are committed to Him.

Clap your hands, shout for joy!
God is real, and He is here!

PSALM 50

God is indeed in our world.
From dawn to dusk,
from twilight hours to the first light
on eastern horizon,
God is near us and around us.

God speaks to our world.
He speaks gently in love
and thunders fiercely in judgment.
He calls to those who are faithful to Him.
He comforts them and challenges them.
He secures them and sends them forth.

God is at work in our world.
He works in and through the lives of His children
     who are loyal and obedient to Him.
"Don't bring your sacrifices to man-made altars
     or build shrines and erect memorials
          on My behalf,"
     He would say to us today.
"I already own the gifts you bring.
All these things have come to you from My hand.
You are to offer them
     on the altar of humanity's need.
These are the sacrifices that get through to Me
     and are accepted by Me."
It is thus that God touches
     the lives of needy men.
It is by way of the self-sacrificing love
     of His servants.

God judges our world.
This judgment falls upon those
     who live totally for themselves.
They are indifferent to the needs
     of their fellowmen.
No matter how impressive their rituals
     and religious exercises,
          their lives are not pleasing to God.

God is in our world.
We serve Him with the kind of worship
     and thanksgiving
     that effectively communicates His love
          to His children in need about us.

PSALM 54

I come in thanksgiving and praise, O God.
Help me to articulate the gratitude
    that I feel toward You.

I was tripped up by my own pride
    and confounded by my foolishness.
I said things and did things that hurt others
    and dishonored You.
I stumbled into a net of my own making
    from which I could not escape.

Then You heard my cries and saw my plight.
You touched me with Your love and set me free
    to walk with You once more.
You continue to deliver me
    from the snares and pitfalls about me.

It is thus that I rejoice, O God.
It is because of this that I offer myself to You.
May Your ever-present love for me
    make me a vehicle of love toward others
      who are troubled and afraid today.

PSALM 55

I am terribly alone, O God,
    and I don't know where to turn.
I thought I was really living
    when I came to the city —
    set free from the restraints
      of childhood and youth.
But now I am frightened.
The people around me are cold and indifferent.
No one knows that I exist.
The traffic by day and the neon glare
    that pushes back the night
      are strange and unfriendly.
I feel as if I am hopelessly lost
    in some concrete wilderness.
The streets lead nowhere —
    except to blend into other streets.
It's a wilderness filled with violence.
Its creatures are dazed, sick, hungry, or angry.
There is oppression and crime and injustice.
There is often blood in the streets.
People are being hurt here in the city.
And one can hardly see the blue sky by day
    or the stars by night
    or hear the song of birds
      or the tolling bells of a church.

It was exciting at first.
I even had a friend with whom to explore
    the mysteries of the city.

Maybe I could have endured
    and found happiness with my friend.
But my friend turned into an enemy.
He no longer needed me
    and melted into the crowds
        that walk down my street.

Then the city became barren and desolate.
The bright lights became ghostly,
    the people about me like walking dead men
        or puppets on a string,
    the clamor and noise hideous and discordant.
And now my soul has become as bleak
    as the city about me.

I am lonely, O God, but I am not alone.
You are here in the city.
O God, help me to find You here in the city.
And enable me, my God,
    to serve You here in the city.

PSALM 72

O God of love,
    grant to Your sons and servants the grace
    to represent you effectively
        in our discordant world.
Give us the courage
    to put our lives on the line
    in communicating life and truth
    to all Your creatures
        wherever they may be found.

Where there is injustice,
may we diagnose its cause
and discover its cure.
Where there is bigotry,
teach us how to love
and how to encourage others to love.
Where there is poverty,
help us to share the wealth
that has come from Your hand.
Where there is war and violence,
may we be peacemakers that lead men
to Your eternal peace.

Help us, O God, to become what You
have destined and empowered us to become.
Where there is darkness,
may we become the rays of Your sun
that banish the gloom of lonely lives.
Where there is drought,
let us be like fresh flowers
that turn barren deserts into green meadows.
Where there is ugliness and distortion,
enable us to portray the beauty and order
of Your will and purposes.

Great God, You are in our world.
Your majesty is reflected
in Your creation about us.
But there are multitudes who do not
feel Your concern or
acknowledge Your love.
Is it because Your servants have failed
to carry out Your command and commission
that we have yet to sense
the significance of our salvation
and the purpose of our mission?

Forbid, O God,
>that we be deaf to the cries of the poor
>and indifferent to those who have needs.
May we identify with those who are oppressed
>and help to bear the burdens
>>of those who suffer about us.
May we hear Your voice of concern
>and feel Your loving touch
>through Your servants who are in this world
>to manifest You to men about them.
The glory is Yours, O God,
>and we shall praise Your name
>and celebrate Your cause together.

PSALM 74

It is disturbing and discouraging, O God,
>to witness the apparent successes
>of those who oppose You.
While Your children wrestle
>with doubts and conflicts,
>the agnostics of our world
>>are tearing down the pillars of our faith
>>and gloating over our frustration.

They have made fun of our rituals and symbols.
They are dissecting our dogmas
>and ridiculing our institutions.
They create godless philosophies
>that seduce the young and confuse the old.
They deliberately obstruct our efforts

to represent You in our world.
As a result of their diabolic activities,
   many are turning away from the true God
      to worship lesser gods
      and to expend their lives on lesser goals.

We know, O God, how You have handled
   Your enemies in the past.
We know that You cannot be dethroned,
   that You are God over all creation.
Then how can You allow these god-defiers
   to get by with what they are doing to us today?

Consider our restlessness, O God.
Do not let us be stepped on and ground under.
Help us, O God,
   ineffective and foolish as we may be,
      to stand up to the demigods
         that plague our land.

PSALMS 75 and 76

We praise You, O God.
Even in the midst of this world's wickedness
   we celebrate Your majesty and power.

For You are here, O God.
You are here to save;
   You are here also to judge.
Even while the godless trumpet their rebellion,
   You hold the world in the palm of Your hand.

Should You close Your hand in anger, O God,
    their doom is sealed,
    their boasts ended forever.

Your fainthearted servants
    need not be dismayed, O God.
Even the rebelliousness of Your obstinate creatures
    can serve to further Your purposes.
We need not fear the distortions
    of those who defy and oppose You.
We need only renew our relationship to You,
    rededicate our lives to Your objectives,
    and continue to celebrate Your presence
    and Your power in our world.

PSALM 80

O God, You are the Creator
    and the Sustainer of Your church.
You have protected and prospered
    Your faithful followers
    throughout the stormy and tumultuous past.

Today we are in trouble.
Listen to our cries of consternation, O God.
We are confused and confounded.
We don't know where to turn,
    in what direction to go.

We have prayed, O God.
We have sung Your praises.

We have proclaimed Your love to the world.
But today our power is slipping away;
      our prestige is wearing thin.
People seem to have little respect for us anymore.
Those who have been brought up
         within our structures
      and have embraced our doctrines
         are leaving the fold.
They say we are no longer meeting their needs
      or the needs of the world.

You were with us in the beginning, Lord.
You planted us in the midst
      of this world's turmoil.
You nurtured us and watched over us.
In spite of Your enemies,
         who sought to destroy us,
         we grew until we encircled the earth.
Great shrines were built in Your honor, Lord.
Magnificent institutions were established
      to carry out Your purposes.
Men dedicated their many skills
      to perpetuate Your teachings.
Multitudes gathered to declare Your praises.

Today we are in trouble, Lord.
The walls are crumbling.
Our sanctuaries no longer attract the masses.
Men's skills are dedicated to other purposes.
We no longer are making much of an impression
      on this world of ours.

Renew Your church, O God.
We know You will never turn away
         those who come to You
      and will forever sustain

those who trust in You.
Fan the dying embers, Lord.
Stir us up, and restore us to the position
of power and effectiveness.
Give us new life and new vision
that we may advance Your kingdom
in our disjointed world.
Renew Your church, O God,
and revive Your servants,
so that the whole earth may know of Your love.

PSALMS 81 and 82

Our great God has heard our cry,
and He is speaking to His church today.
I hear Him saying many things.
He reminds us that He is God,
that He is in our world,
that He is the same God
who guided His people throughout history,
that He continues to regard His church
with love and concern.
He would have us remember
how He freed us from sin's burden and guilt,
how He responded to our pleas for deliverance
and was present with us
in the trials and conflicts of our lives.
He brings to our remembrance the many times
we neglected to listen to Him
and how He had to allow us to hurt ourselves
because we stubbornly chose our own course.
He reiterates His promise to meet our needs

and to enrich our lives
    as we rely on Him for grace and strength.
He diagnoses our sickness even today
    and points us to His purpose for our existence.

We have become complacent
    in our structures and institutions.
We have been subtly diverted
    from His will and purposes in our world.
We have selfishly interpreted His Word
    to fit our schemes and carry out our intents.
We have clutched at God to pacify and sustain us
    even while we remain insensitive
        to the suffering world about us.

Now God is speaking again,
    in judgment as well as with promise.
He is reaching out to restore us to Himself
    and to renew our vision for His world.
"How long will you ignore
    My oppressed and dispossessed children,
    their cries for liberty and justice?"
        our God is saying to the church.
"Why are there people going hungry about you
    while you abound in the gifts
        that come from My hand?
You are My sons and servants,
    My representatives in a fractured world.
I can reach those sick, needy, loveless,
    and lonely creatures only through you.
This is the reason I have given you so much,
    that you may share it with them."

Help us, O God,
    to return to Your purposes for Your church,
    to recognize all men as Your subjects,

that the world belongs to You.
May Your great love flood our lives
　　only to overflow and touch with healing
　　and to channel Your grace to the lives
　　　of every one of Your children.

You are in our world, O God.
May we serve You here by ministering
　　to the needs of our fellowmen.

PSALM 85

O God, You have indeed been good to us.
You have prospered our land.
You have opened Your heart to us in love.
You have forgiven our sins
　　and adopted us as Your sons.

But now our country is in turmoil.
We no longer have confidence in our leaders.
Our citizens are in revolt.
Our young men are spilling their blood
　　in foreign wars.
People are turning away from You
　　and are being ensnared
　　　by strange doctrines
　　　and godless philosophies.

We know that You have not turned away from us.
You touch with joy and peace
　　the hearts that are open to You.
You stand ready to show Your salvation.

to all who will trust in You.
As we speak to You in faith,
    You respond in loving concern.
You will give us what is good
    and will prosper us
        with gifts from Your hand.
You are holy and just.
You love Your children
    and will guide them
        in Your course for their lives.

Renew our faith, O God.
Forgive us our many failures and infidelities.
May our land continue to be a place
    where we can be free to love and serve You.

PSALM 92

It's a glorious feeling to be able
    to unload my heart,
    to spill out my gratitude
        in thanks to You, O God.
Morning, noon, and night
    I want the whole world to know of Your love.
I want to shout it, to sing it,
    in every possible way
        to proclaim Your praises,
        to express my joy.

How great You are, O Lord!
Your thoughts are unfathomable,
    Your ways beyond comprehension.

And all the while we are still confounded
    over the problem of evil.
We simply cannot understand
    why the ungodly appear to be so successful,
    why good fortune seems to follow those
        who defy You.
But we know their success is short lived.
Those who refuse to turn to You will never find
    that ultimate and total fulfillment
        that is promised to the sons of God.

The children of God,
    those who open their lives to You,
        portray the wonder and beauty of Your Spirit.
They are like springs of water in a parched world.
They flourish even amid the distortions
    and the ugliness around them.
Their lives are rich and productive
    in a barren and desolate society.

Help us, those of us who love You, O God,
    to prove to our disjointed world
        that You are in our midst.

PSALM 96

God is here; God is now!
It is a time for celebration!
Our praises need not be confined to old songs.
Nor need we great organs or massive choirs
    to honor His name.
Let us create new songs of praise to our God.

Let us discover new ways of proclaiming
    His greatness and glory.

The elements about us reflect His majesty.
The roaring sea and all that inhabits it,
    the wind that bends the trees,
    the creatures that fill the air and land,
    the mountains that probe our skies,
    the rivers and lakes that slake our thirst,
    the great planets and stars
      that light up our night:
    all these reveal
      the beauty and splendor of God.
And out of this comes that fashioned
    by man's mind and hand:
      rockets and computers,
      art and architecture,
      music and literature.

Wherever one turns,
    God's power is manifested,
    God's presence is made apparent.
Let us celebrate His presence
    in our world today.

PSALM 98

Men have proclaimed God's praises
    throughout the ages.
Now it is our turn to worship the Lord
    and to announce God's presence
    and His loving concern

for the inhabitants of this world.
His power is as great today as it ever was.
He continues to reign over His universe
    and the creatures that move in this world.
He alone is the true God.
He offers to all men His salvation.
He is close to His sons and servants
    and fills the hearts of His children with joy.

Now, as His sons and servants,
    let us express this joy.
With voice and musical instruments,
    with lovely melodies and joyful sounds,
        let us proclaim the glory of God.
Let us fill our homes and sanctuaries,
    our halls of learning,
    our factories and marketplaces,
    even the streets of our city,
        with sounds of celebration.
God is here; God is now!

PSALM 111

My heart is full today.
I am so grateful
    for all that God has done for me.
I need but crawl out of my corner
        of depression and self-pity
    and look around me to see
        how great my God is.

I cannot see Him,
    but I can see the works of His hands.
He is a merciful and loving God.
How tenderly He deals with those
    whose hearts are open to Him!
He is a righteous and faithful God.
His promises and precepts are forever.
He is a majestic and powerful God.
He created me and sustains me day by day.
He is a forgiving God.
He takes me back to His loving heart
    when I go astray.
He is in this world today.
And those who recognize and accept His presence
    are building on foundations
      that are eternally secure.
How grateful I am to my God today!

PSALM 112

What about the man who trusts in God
    and is committed
      to His will and purposes?

He is a man who is rich indeed.
Even amid the circumstances of poverty,
    the wealth and blessings of God
      are within his reach.
He is a man with purpose and meaning in his life.
Even amid the disorder and void
    of this temporal existence,
    he is aware of God's concern and love for him.

He is a man who walks unafraid.
The threats of violence or prophecies of doom
        do not detract from his validity
            nor alter his course.
He is a man who relates to his fellow beings.
He identifies with them
            in their sorrows and complaints
        and shares with them his life and his gifts.

He is the man who is truly happy
        and through whom our God is working out
            His purposes in this world today.

PSALM 113

How great and glorious is our God!
From hour to hour, from day to day
        our lives ought to overflow
            with praise and gratitude.
It is amazing, even fantastic,
        how our God permeates every facet of our lives
        and can work out His purposes through them
            despite our human faults and failures.

He creates beauty out of the dust
        of our fallen natures.
Out of the ashes of our failures
        He brings forth meaning and purpose.
He exalts the humble and enriches the poor.
He transforms our weaknesses
        into channels of strength.
Our emptiness becomes

a vessel of His fullness,
our spiritual poverty the basis
for His eternal grace.
Our errors and mistakes
are stepping-stones to success.
Our defeats are but incidents
on the road to victory.

But this is God's doing, not ours.
How great and glorious is our God!

PSALM 116

I know that God is here.
I know this because,
when I laid bare my soul
and stood naked before Him,
He looked upon me with love
and responded to my cry for help.

There was a time when I didn't care
whether He was here or not.
I was not aware of any particular need for Him.
But then I hit bottom.
Death itself reached out to embrace me.
There was no one else to turn to.
I cried out to God in my desperation.
I could almost feel His invisible hand
encircle me and draw me to Himself.

Now I am convinced.
God is here, and I shall trust Him forever.

I will no longer wait for pain or suffering
    to drive me to Him.
I will walk in His course for my life.
I am committed to His purposes,
    and I intend to carry out that commitment.

I can never repay my God
    for His ever-present love.
I can only dedicate my life
    to praising Him
    and to serving Him wherever I may be.
I am His servant and His son,
    and I shall love Him forever.
I shall proclaim to all the world
    that God is in our midst.

PSALMS 127 and 128

Man's struggle for significance
    apart from God's will and purposes
        is in vain.
Man builds homes and institutions;
    he acquires property and possessions;
    he crowds the cities with the clutter
        of questionable achievements;
    he fills the better part of every day
        with self-centered activities;
    he pushes and prods in an anxiety-ridden quest
        for some ephemeral treasure;
    he strives incessantly to get to the top.
And all the while worth and value
    are within him

or very close to him.
They are the precious gifts of God
    that come in some measure to all men.

There are visible evidences of a man's worth:
    the children he begets,
    the beloved mate that brings him joy,
    the ability to supply
      his own and his family's needs
        through his daily labors.
But even beyond this and long before this,
    a man's true worth was established
      by God Himself.

PSALM 145

God is here — let's celebrate!
Let us enlist our lives in perpetual celebration
    over God's goodness and greatness.
Let us announce to the world God's presence
      and proclaim His loving concern for all men.

How compassionate He is over all
    that He has created,
   how tender and loving
    toward His failure-fraught creatures!
He will not cop out on His promises to us.
His blessings are not reserved only for those
    who fit obediently into His design for them.
He is just — and He is forgiving.
He gently picks up those who have fallen
    and restores them to sonship and servanthood.

He sustains those who are wavering in weakness
    and grants them His grace and strength.
He reaches into the void of empty lives
    and enriches and fulfills their hungry hearts.
He is near enough to hear our every cry,
    to sense our every need,
    to grant us whatever is necessary
    to make us happy and productive
        as we seek to follow and to serve Him.

How incomparably glorious is our great God!
May our mouths articulate
    and our lives demonstrate
    His ever-present love
        for all the creatures of our world.
Let us celebrate
    the eternal mercy and goodness of our God.